EXPERIENCE EASTER

DAILY DEVOTIONS AND REFLECTIONS ON THE EASTER STORY

Jennifer Carter

Hope Books Ltd

Hope Books Ltd, Windover House, St. Ann Street, Salisbury SP1 2DR
www.jennifer-carter.com

Book Layout ©2015 BookDesignTemplates.com

Edited by Daphne Parsekian

Experience Easter / Jennifer Carter. -- 1st ed.
ISBN 978-1-908567-32-1

Contents

this book is dedicated to
fellow-travellers Lena, Sara and Catherine

"A dead Christ I must do everything for; a living Christ does everything for me."

— ANDREW MURRAY

Introduction

The amazing truth and explosive power of the Christian message is to be found in the Easter story.

It's here, that we see Jesus' love clearly revealed for us.

Yet there's a danger that we can become all too familiar with the Easter story, even take it for granted. We can become inured to the graphic details of all that took place during Holy Week—Jesus's betrayal, crucifixion, death, burial, and resurrection.

If you've never heard it before, its during Holy Week that you can see Jesus' love most clearly revealed.

Yet in every step of Jesus, each story and new vista, there is something to be astonished at afresh. This is truly a story to be in awe of, a story to discover anew.

Jesus himself spoke many times to His disciples about His rejection, suffering and death. He promised them that on the third day He would be raised to life.

The writers of the gospels unashamedly devoted much of their writing to tell us, in great detail, of Jesus' final days and hours.

Paul, the Apostle, encouraged us to "know Christ and Him crucified" (1 Cor. 2:2). He spoke of preaching "Christ crucified" (1 Cor. 1:23), emphasising that the crucifixion is at the very heart of the Christian faith—that understanding Jesus Christ, His crucifixion, and His resurrection is central to our understanding of the good news of Jesus.

As we share together by reading through the Bible and look deeper into the happenings of Easter week, be prepared for God to reveal Himself to you in a new way.

Walk with Jesus along the rough road to Jerusalem, and join the crowds as they welcome Him with hosannas. See Him as he faces accusation, betrayal, and humiliation; shares a last meal with His friends; and prays in the garden of Gethsemane whilst awaiting betrayal.

Look on during the final agonising hours of His suffering and gruesome crucifixion. Watch as the disciples are transformed when they meet the resurrected Jesus and finally understand who He is.

As we unravel the truth of the Easter story together, let's look closely at this incredible Saviour.

We can look on in awe and wonder as we witness the struggle and pain of Jesus—as we grasp the joy and deliverance experienced by His disciples, both then and now.

It takes courage to experience Easter.

As we immerse ourselves in the Easter story, embrace the foot of the cross, watch as the sharp splinters of wood pierce His hands, look on as His precious, life-giving blood drips from His broken body. I truly believe we will never be the same again.

Are you ready to be changed by the Easter experience?

CHAPTER ONE

The Third Day

"How can the guests of the bridegroom fast while he is with them? They cannot, so long as they have him with them. But the time will come when the bridegroom will be taken from them" Mark 2:19–20 (NIV)

"He then began to teach them that the Son of Man must suffer many things and be rejected by the elders, the chief priests and the teachers of the law, and that he must be killed and after three days rise again." Mark 8:31 (NIV)
"He told them very clearly what he meant.." Mark 8:32 (GOD'S WORD)

"'Remember how he told you back in Galilee that he had to be handed over to sinners, killed on a cross, in three days rise up?' Then they remembered Jesus words." Luke 24:6–8 (The Message)

Jesus clearly knew and taught his followers all that was about to happen to Him. The disciples shouldn't have been taken by surprise by all that was about to happen to Jesus. Since the beginning, He had been teaching and preparing them for His final days.

The disciples walked daily with Jesus as He expounded the Scriptures throughout Galilee and Judea. They listened intently as He spoke in synagogues, to crowds on hillsides, and to individuals they met as they travelled. Yet nothing could prepare them for the swiftness of events, Jesus' betrayal, the venomous plot against Him, the injustice of his trial, and the brutality of His death. They simply didn't see it coming.

Again and again, Jesus spoke clearly and in detail about all that would happen to Him in Jerusalem. He predicted it all, every terrible detail —His betrayal, painful death, and resurrection. He didn't speak in metaphors or parables but clearly outlined His final days and hours.

Early in His ministry, Jesus was clear about what was going to happen. He proclaimed "Destroy this temple, and I will raise it again in three days" (John 2:19 NIV) to the Jews who were looking for a sign.

Even as He hung on the cross, Jesus was pointing His followers to the Scriptures that foretold of this moment with His words "My God, my God, why have you forsaken me?" from Psalm 22.

It was such common knowledge—although seemingly not to His disciples—amongst the Jewish leaders in Jerusalem that Jesus had said He would rise to life that this was the very reason they asked Pilate to place a guard at the tomb.

"'Sir,' they said, 'we remember that while he was still alive that deceiver said, "After three days I will rise again."'" Matthew 27:63 (NIV)

The disciples believed they had a measure of understanding of Jesus' purpose. On the road to Emmaus, two of his friends walked unknowingly with Him, talking of their hopes that "he was the Messiah who had come to rescue Israel (Luke 24:21 NLT).

Only as Jesus pointed out the scriptures that refer to Him were the disciples' eyes finally opened to the truth, and they recognised that it was Jesus who had been walking with them. Excitedly, they returned to tell their fellow disciples how He "explained the Scriptures to us" (Luke 24:32 NLT).

Jesus clearly tried to prepare the disciples for His coming death and resurrection. Yet in the final hours, it was the Jewish leaders who had had Him crucified who remembered His words most clearly, whilst his disciples fled in fear. Not an encouraging start for these men in the first hours of their trial. As the story continues, we see God's plan unfolding.

Despite their weaknesses, we discover that God had a plan and purpose for these disciples. These chosen men, who at times were hesitant, slow to believe, and weak in faith would come to understand all that God had been doing, both in their lives and as part of His eternal plan.

These same men would be transformed after meeting the risen Jesus. They'd become fearless after being filled with the Holy Spirit. They became courageous, able and willing to suffer for who and what they believed in. They became world-changing messengers taking the good news about Jesus to the nations of the world.

Reflection

Father, thank you that Jesus knew everything that would happen to Him and yet He still came. Thank you that He died and rose again.

Thank you that you alone have the words of eternal life. Thank you that every word I read in the Bible is true.

Thank you that You alone are the fountain of Truth and Wisdom.

Help me to listen to and hear Your words. Let your truth break in and change me.

Grant me wisdom as I seek to follow and honour You. Plant your Word deep in my heart so that it will strengthen and comfort me in times of trial.

CHAPTER TWO

The Lonely Walk of the Ransomed Son

"And they were in the way going up to Jerusalem; and Jesus went before them: and they were amazed; and as they followed, they were afraid. And he took again the twelve, and began to tell them what things should happen to him, Saying, Behold, we go up to Jerusalem; and the Son of man shall be delivered to the chief priests, and to the scribes; and they shall condemn him to death, and shall deliver him to the Gentiles: And they shall mock him, and shall whip him, and shall spit on him, and shall kill him: and the third day he shall rise again." Mark 10:32–34 (KJV)

"He came to serve and to give his life as a ransom for many." Matthew 20:28 (NASB)

As he climbed the rocky path to Jerusalem, it was astonishing to see Jesus leading the way.

"Jesus went before them...they followed."
Mark 10:32 (KJV)

He knew exactly what was ahead of Him, yet unbelievably, He led the way. He didn't slow down but rather sped up.

We read elsewhere that Jesus set His face like flint for Jerusalem. We can only imagine what the disciples were thinking. Just a few moments before they were arguing over who would be greatest in the Kingdom.

As they climbed towards Jerusalem, a change came over the face of their beloved master. Determined and courageous, Jesus led the way up to Jerusalem, towering above the surrounding landscape. No wonder the disciples looked amazed and afraid.

This perfect man strode boldly towards a scourging; this royal King was about to be treated as a criminal. The one to whom all honour and glory is due would be subjected to mocking and spitting. The one in whom we can place our trust would be betrayed, and He who brings abundant life would be put to death.

The Messiah to the Jews would be handed over to the Gentiles and be given over to the very Roman soldiers the people had hoped He would overthrow.

Yet, knowing all this, Jesus didn't slow down but sped up. Knowing His identity and the fate that awaited Him, He led the way on the rough road up to Jerusalem.

It was as if He was looking past those next few days to the end goal. As the ransom payer, the ransom in person, Jesus fixed

His eyes on something other than what we or the disciples can see at this point.

Before they arrived in the City, Jesus paused and took time with his disciples, telling them once again of the fate that awaited Him.

Both Jesus and the disciples had already heard the scribes and Pharisees discuss arresting Him. Even so, perhaps the disciples hoped for some miraculous escape, an overcoming of their Roman oppressors and the religious authorities who opposed him.

On His lonely march to buy our freedom, we see another side to Jesus. Even His close friends, those who knew Him best, were amazed yet also afraid. Maybe as they walked up the rockstrewn mountain road, it was dawning on them that perhaps Jesus wouldn't be the conquering hero in quite the way they had expected.

Perhaps something about His countenance changed. This was a man who was fixed in His course, a man whose calm resolve had his friends, the disciples, at a loss for words.

As He left the shores of Galilee for the City of Jerusalem, this gentle healer and truth speaker focused on His role as our ransom.

It was as if everything He faced was simply an obstacle to His one great goal.

Instead of pain, Jesus saw freedom-giving. Instead of death, He saw the power of resurrection life. Instead of shame, He saw the freedom and redemption that He would purchase. Instead of betrayal, He offered Himself, the Faithful One. Even the division between Jews and Gentiles He broke down with each determined step towards Jerusalem.

It was as if Jesus was living out the parable that He had told not so long before of a father running to greet his lost son. It was as if He couldn't wait to get to Jerusalem and to the cross to set us free.

We are privileged to witness one man's long walk to purchase our freedom. After more than thirty years on this earth, Jesus strode out towards the culmination of His Mission, ready to pay the full price—no matter what the cost.

Reflection

Thank you for Jesus' willing sacrifice. Thank you that—knowing all that you faced—you went willingly to the cross for me. Thank you that you payed the ransom for my sins.

I'm amazed that, knowing everything, you still chose to go to Jerusalem to face persecution and death.

Thank you for so willingly and resolutely paying the ransom to set me free.

Help me to live in the power of the freedom and life that Jesus purchased for me.

CHAPTER THREE

Heir & Tenants

And he began to speak to them in parables. "A man planted a vineyard and put a fence around it and dug a pit for the wine press and built a tower, and leased it to tenants and went into another country. When the season came, he sent a servant to the tenants to get from them some of the fruit of the vineyard. And they took him and beat him and sent him away empty-handed. Again he sent to them another servant, and they struck him on the head and treated him shamefully. And he sent another, and him they killed. And so with many others: some they beat, and some they killed. He had still one other, a beloved son. Finally he sent him to them, saying, 'They will respect my son.' But those tenants said to one another, 'This is the heir. Come, let us kill him, and the inheritance will be ours.' And they took him and killed him and threw him out of the vineyard. What will the owner of the vineyard do? He will come and destroy the tenants and give the vineyard to others. Have you not read this Scripture:

"'The stone that the builders rejected has become the cornerstone;

this was the Lord's doing and it is marvellous in our eyes'?"

And they were seeking to arrest him but feared the people, for they perceived that he had told the parable against them. So they left him and went away. Mark 12:1–12 (ESV, Anglicised)

Jesus told this parable following His triumphant entry into the city of Jerusalem after the cleansing of the temple. As these momentous events in history drew to a close, it seems fair to assume that any story Jesus told at this time must have tremendous significance.

The disciples may still have been anticipating Jesus to triumph, as their Messiah, over the Romans and the authorities. What Jesus told in this story reveals that this could hardly be further from the truth of what is about to unfold.

Jesus told this parable of a landowner who entrusts his vineyard to tenants. He told of a landowner who has provided everything to prepare for the fruitfulness of his land. Vines are planted, fencing erected, a pit prepared for the winepress and a tower built.

It's probably clear to any listener to the story what was owed to the man who planted the vineyard: a share in a bountiful harvest.

At harvest time, when the landowner rightly expected to collect the rent, he sends his servants to make the collection. The twist in the tale is that not only do they not receive any payment but they are treated harshly. The first is beaten, then one is killed, and yet another is stoned.

Finally, the landowner sends his son, thinking surely they will respect his son. Yet these deluded tenants, talking among themselves, believe that if they kill the heir, his inheritance will be theirs. Instead of honouring the son, they murder him.

They foolishly fail to realise that killing the son means there has to be a day of reckoning. The landowner himself must surely respond to such treachery and betrayal.

Jesus told this parable against those chief priests, scribes, and leaders—the ones who had been entrusted with leading the Jewish people. Even as He told this parable, He knew that in a few days, He himself would be betrayed. Instead of honouring the Son of God, these religious leaders would kill him brutally on a cross.

Once again, Jesus, knowing all that would happen to him, predicted His own imminent death. He clearly talked of himself as the son of the landowner, here representing God, His Father.

In the parable, the final acts of the tenants was that they cast him out of the vineyard and killed him. This is exactly what happened just a few days later as Jesus carried His cross and was crucified outside Jerusalem's city walls.

Jesus gave us a hint of the ending of the story when He read the scriptures that say, "the Stone which the builders rejected has become the chief Cornerstone" (1 Peter 2:7 WEB). He was clearly talking about being raised to His rightful place as Son of God following His rejection by the Jewish leaders.

As He related this parable to His listeners, Jesus had a perfect understanding of what awaited Him. Yet He was calm and perfectly submitted to the will of His Father.

Just a few days after Jesus told this story, His followers would be able to look back on the events that had taken place and finally grasp the fullness of all that Jesus had told them.

It was so memorable a moment for them that it was recorded by three of the gospel writers: Mark, Matthew, and Luke. Though they didn't understand fully at the time, later their eyes were opened to the truth that Jesus revealed about Himself.

The religious leaders of the day failed to listen to Jesus and turn around. These chief priests, scribes, and Jewish leaders were afraid, not of Jesus and what He revealed about their hearts or about the way they wielded political power, but of the people.

Instead of taking the opportunity to change their lives, they responded with fear—not fear of the Messiah standing in front of them but of the reaction of the people should they try to arrest Jesus and their fear of losing political power.

Their hardened hearts made them unable to see and hear Jesus, the very embodiment of truth, even when He was standing in front of them.

The parable shows us two extreme reactions to Jesus: the disciples, who are clearly powerfully impacted, and the religious leaders, whose hardened hearts made them incapable of understanding and responding to truth.

Even today reactions to Jesus are split into two extremes: those whose hearts are hardened and those who sit at His feet, ready to listen and respond to His voice.

Reflection

Father, help me to hear you speak.

Please send your Holy Spirit to soften my heart and show me where my heart has become hardened.

Even now I bring to you those areas where my heart has become hard to you and to others. Forgive me, and fill me afresh with your Holy Spirit. I long to hear your voice.

Give me faith and courage. Faith to know that it is you who touches hearts. Courage to speak to people about Jesus and to allow you to reach those whose hearts you have already softened with your words. Help me not to fear discouragement but to trust Your perfect plan.

CHAPTER FOUR

A Day Pregnant
With Meaning

"The blood you have placed on the doorposts will be proof that you obey me, and when I see the blood I will pass over you and I will not destroy your firstborn children when I smite the land of Egypt." Exodus 12:13 (TLB)

"It is the celebration of Jehovah's passing over us, for he passed over the homes of the people of Israel, though he killed the Egyptians; he passed over our houses and did not come in to destroy us." Exodus 12:27 (TLB)

"The Passover observance began two days later—an annual Jewish holiday when no bread made with yeast was eaten. The chief priests and other Jewish leaders were still looking for an opportunity to arrest Jesus secretly and put him to death." Mark 14:1 (TLB)

The exact timing of Jesus' death was no coincidence. It's timing was perfect and quite remarkable. His death and resurrection during the annual celebration of the Passover and the Feast of Unleavened Bread holds great significance.

The Passover celebrations reminded the Israelites of God's deliverance from their oppression in Egypt. At this time, more than any other, people were aware of and expectant for the coming Messiah. They hoped a Messiah would free them from Roman tyranny.

It was a time of remembering God's past goodness to them and looking forward to His release and intervention once again.

It was the time when they remembered their cruel oppression under four hundred years of slavery. It commemorates the raising up of Moses, whom God used to deliver them and set them free.

If ever there was a time when the people should've been joyful and full of grace, it was during the Passover, when they remembered al that God had done for them.

It is into this point in history, a religious holiday celebrating freedom, that Jesus came.

He knew that the Passover foreshadowed the very events that were about to take place. He knew He was the fulfilment of prophecy and understood the true meaning of the Passover. He himself became the Passover lamb, the innocent one killed to purchase the freedom of a people in need of deliverance.

The Passover celebrations in Jerusalem were spread over seven days. They focused on the Passover sacrifice and meal following the slaughter of a pure lamb. All the men in the surrounding villages were expected to attend the celebrations. Men from farther afield, including Galilee and Nazareth, would also have been encouraged to make the pilgrimage to celebrate the Passover in Jerusalem.

"Then came the first day of Unleavened Bread on which the Passover lamb had to be sacrificed. And Jesus sent Peter and John, saying, "Go and prepare the Passover for us, so that we may eat it." "(Luke 22:7–8 NASB)

This day that Jesus was betrayed was the very day when all of Jerusalem celebrated their deliverance from years of oppression in Egypt.

The Passover meal had always held a deep significance for the Jewish people. As the disciples prepared the Passover, little did they know that the Passover traditions they had known all their lives were about to be turned upside down. A new meaning to Passover would soon be revealed.

The Passover meal itself commemorates the bringing out of God's people, their deliverance and redemption. It reminds the people of their identity as a nation that God loves and has chosen for His purposes. Jesus' every action during the meal carried meaning.

As Jesus lifted the cup and gave thanks, they remembered the blood of innocent lambs, which, spread on the doorposts of their homes in Egypt, brought them redemption from slavery.

As Jesus broke the bread and uttered the words "This is my body, which is given for you," His meaning was clear. He himself was the innocent lamb whose slaughter would bring freedom for His people.

As Jesus speaks the words of the Psalms, He speaks of the goodness of God.

The disciples' eyes must have finally began to understand that the victory they had been anticipating was going to look very different from all that they had expected and hoped.

What seems hardest, almost impossible, to understand is that those Jewish people, who on this very night celebrated the hard-won freedom from slavery and oppression, would be the same ones in the crowd shouting, "Crucify him!" They'd free Barabbas, a murderer, and send Jesus, an innocent man, the Son of God, to the cross. Whilst embracing the truth of the Passover with their minds, it failed to touch their hearts and change their lives.

We are given a glimpse into our own state without God's re-demptive power—the darkness of our hearts, the blindness of our eyes, the foolishness of our minds, and the flaws inherent in our fallen nature.

Whilst some believe that man is inherently good, this story reveals that man, at his core, is inherently flawed. Yet Jesus, our innocent Passover lamb, knowing our need of deliverance, died for us and purchased our freedom.

Let's never forget the freedom that has been purchased for us. To remember always that we ourselves have been redeemed by the suffering and blood of an innocent man. That whilst once we were oppressed and in slavery, now we have been set free by our great deliverer, Jesus.

Reflection

Father, thank you so much for the freedom you purchased for me. Thank you that I was once a slave but am now set free.

Soften my heart, open my eyes, give me your wisdom, and transform my mind—make me more like Jesus.

Today, help me to live out and share that beautiful, costly freedom that Jesus purchased for me on the cross. Help me to act with grace and love to those I meet as I rejoice in the freedom that You won for me.

CHAPTER SIX

Pure Nard

Now the Passover and the Festival of Unleavened Bread were only two days away, and the chief priests and the teachers of the law were scheming to arrest Jesus secretly and kill him. "But not during the festival," they said, "or the people may riot."

While he was in Bethany, reclining at the table in the home of Simon the Leper, a woman came with an alabaster jar of very expensive perfume, made of pure nard. She broke the jar and poured the perfume on his head.

Some of those present were saying indignantly to one another, "Why this waste of perfume? It could have been sold for more than a year's wages and the money given to the poor." And they rebuked her harshly.

"Leave her alone," said Jesus. "Why are you bothering her? She has done a beautiful thing to me. The poor you will always have with you, and you can help them any time you want. But you will not always have me. She did what she could. She poured perfume

on my body beforehand to prepare for my burial. Truly I tell you, wherever the gospel is preached throughout the world, what she has done will also be told, in memory of her." Mark 14:1–9 (NIV)

Here we are privileged to see a beautiful moment as Jesus prepared for His crucifixion. As He was sharing a meal with His friends and disciples, a woman came to honour and express her love for Jesus in an unprecedented way. She walks into the room, interrupting their conversation and meal to pour perfume over His head.

Her offering was extravagant. The beautiful alabaster jar contained pure nard, an expensive perfume so valuable that in those days, it was the equivalent of a family's savings or pension plan.

Once the slim neck of the jar was broken, there was no going back; the perfume must be poured out. The value of the perfume was worth a years' wages.

What extravagance! This was an honest and heartfelt demonstration of respect and honour. A pouring out of love for Jesus.

For once we see Jesus receiving from someone. He's usually the one who is giving, but here Jesus not only allowed her to bless Him in this way but He even praised her for it. It somehow seems appropriate that as Jesus set His face to the cross, it was a humble woman who brought a moment of beauty at such a dark time.

In John 12:3 (TLB), we read, "Mary took a jar of costly perfume made from essence of nard, and anointed Jesus' feet with it and wiped them with her hair. And the house was filled with fragrance."

Both Mark and John relate the diverse responses this action elicited from those in the room with Jesus, clearly revealing the state of their hearts.

Judas spoke out about the waste and complained that the money could have been better used. Judas' comments stirred up the other disciples, who responded with criticism, indignation, and rebuke. They were indignant and angry at this interruption to their meal. They looked on at this act of worship and saw waste and unnecessary extravagance.

Jesus told them to leave her alone, saying that she had done a good thing. Though she could not have realised the full significance of her actions, Jesus said that this woman had anointed His body for burial ahead of time.

Jesus words, "She has done what she could," are powerful. These words remind us of what we read in 1 Samuel 14:7 (ESV): "Do all that is in your heart." Mary followed the leading of her heart, pouring out this perfume on Jesus' head.

Jesus saw an act of such significance, of such worth, that what she did will be preached throughout the world wherever the good news is preached.

Mary, focused on Jesus, chose to bring Him joy, neither thinking nor caring what others might think or say. She knew that she would face criticism for her action, but rather than being concerned about the words of the men around the table, she chose to follow her heart to serve her Master.

This woman's unconditional love is what makes this story so beautiful. This act is an outpouring from her heart, her thankfulness for all that Jesus is and had done for her.

Her timing was perfect. Looking back through history, we can see that this was Jesus' anointing for burial. Only days later, Jesus' body would be lying in a cold tomb.

Maybe this beautiful perfume still clung to Jesus' body and hair as He hung on the cross. Maybe as he stood trial before Pilate and Herod the sweet fragrance perfumed the air.

We can never know the full significance or impact of our actions. All we need to know is that if we are following the leading of our hearts as we seek to follow Jesus and bless and serve those around us, we can trust that He will use us to spread the wonderful fragrance of Jesus.

Reflection

Father, thank you that you love me unconditionally. Thank you for your determination to go through with a painful death to purchase my freedom.

As Mary broke and poured out that perfume, there was no going back. Help me to hold nothing back from you but to give all that I have to you. Help me to open my heart to release all that I have to you, not holding back but giving freely.

Lead me and stir my heart to do what I can to show your love, compassion, and extravagance to those around me. May you love others through me, bringing your beautiful fragrance into their lives.

CHAPTER SEVEN

The Hallel Psalms (Psalms 113–118)

"Praise the LORD!
Praise, O servants of the LORD,
Praise the name of the LORD.
Blessed be the name of the LORD
From this time forth and forever.
From the rising of the sun to its setting
The name of the LORD is to be praised."
Psalm 113:1–3 (NASB)

"The Lord is gracious and righteous;
our God is full of compassion."
Psalm 116:5 (NIV)

The psalms sing the praises of God, and they remind us of who He is. The Jewish people used words from the psalms as prayers and songs, just as they are used today.

At the Last Supper, the disciples' final meal with Jesus, it is likely that it was the Hallel Psalms that were sung. According to

Jewish tradition, they would have been recited or sung by those sitting around the table.

The Hallel Psalms refer to Psalms 113 to 118. 'Hallel' is the Hebrew word for praise. These psalms are unstinting and unreserved in their praise of God. These words, sung or spoken every year at Passover, speak of salvation, of triumph, and of God's grace and love for his people.

As Jesus prepared both himself and His disciples for His imminent death and crucifixion, singing praises is an unlikely choice. In our minds, perhaps we think that one of David's psalms that speaks of struggle and God's ultimate victory would seem more appropriate.

Yet it is these psalms, liberal in their praise of God, that are sung at Jesus' final meal with His friends.

Instead of weeping, He sings. Instead of being fearful, He extols the praises of His Father.

"Not to us, LORD, not to us but to your name be the glory, because of your love and faithfulness." Psalm 115:1 (NIV)

"I love the LORD, for he heard my voice; he heard my cry for mercy." Psalm 116:1 (NIV)

"I will lift up the cup of salvation and call on the name of the LORD.
I will fulfil my vows to the LORD in the presence of all his people." Psalm 116:13–14 (NIV)

As He was about to drink the most difficult cup of all, as He brought us salvation by taking our sins on Himself at the cross, He spoke of calling on the name of the LORD.

"I will sacrifice a thank offering to you and call on the name of the LORD.
I will fulfil my vows to the LORD in the presence of all his people,
In the court of the house of the LORD—in your midst, Jerusalem." Psalm 116:17–19 (NIV)

How poignant these words sound as we know that Jesus himself was soon to be tried and put to death and sacrificed on a cross with crowds of onlookers right in Jerusalem. These words speak of a 'thank offering', of fulfilling vows.

"Praise the LORD, all you nations;
extol him, all you peoples.
For great is his love toward us,
and the faithfulness of the LORD endures forever.
Praise the LORD."
Psalm 117:1-2 (NIV)

As He looked towards His final hours, it seems almost inconceivable to us that it is not on His own suffering that He was focusing. These words speak of praise, of the love and faithfulness of His Father.

Aware of all that will unfold over the next few hours, Jesus fixed His eyes on the goodness of His Father.

"The LORD is with me; I will not be afraid.
What can mere mortals do to me?

The LORD is with me; he is my helper.
I look in triumph on my enemies."
Psalm 118:6–7 (NIV)

The words speak of triumphing over enemies, speaking from the viewpoint of having accomplished all that He had been sent to do.

It is almost as if, even though He had yet to walk the painful path to Calvary, He was looking at these events from the standpoint of eternity, looking back and seeing all He had accomplished. Instead of considering the suffering He was to endure from this point on, Jesus took an eternal perspective and looked forward to the joy that He would soon know.

"The stone the builders rejected has become the cornerstone; the LORD has done this, and it is marvelous in our eyes."
Psalm 118:22–23 (NIV)

It is these very words that Jesus spoke shortly after he arrived in Jerusalem for the Passover, after telling the parable of the tenants. It was these inflammatory words that caused the chief priests, the teachers of the law, and the elders to start looking for a way to arrest Him. It was these very men, who considered themselves the 'builders' of Jerusalem, who rejected Jesus and His claims.

The Hallel Psalms end with these uplifting words:

"You are my God, and I will praise you; you are my God, and I will exalt you. Give thanks to the LORD, for he is good; his love endures forever." Psalm 118:28–29 (NIV)

These may have been the final words from the Bible that Jesus uttered whilst with His disciples that night. He doesn't speak, as we might expect, of fear, of shame, or of death. Instead, He speaks of the goodness of God and the enduring nature of His love. Jesus focused on praise, on His Father, on His goodness and His faithfulness.

By changing our focus, we can help conquer our fears. Instead of focusing on ourselves, on what we face and have to endure, we can make a choice to focus on the Father, on His character, and on His goodness. We can know that one day - we will know unending joy in His presence.

Reflection

Father, thank you that knowing all He had to face, Jesus gave praise and thanks to you.

Help me to see my life through your eyes, through the perspective of eternity.

In the challenges I face, help me to fix my eyes on you. Thank you that you are good and that your love endures forever. Thank you that you are always with me, that you are my helper.

Thank you for the promise that one day I will look in triumph over my enemies—over those who mock and harm me now, who criticise and judge, and who speak harsh words or hurt me.

I'm so thankful that your Word says that you hear my cry for mercy because you love me. I choose now to trust in your love and faithfulness today.

Holy Spirit, strengthen and empower me to look away from my circumstances and up at the Father. Help me to walk in trust and obedience today.

CHAPTER EIGHT

For the Joy Set Before Him

"My soul is exceeding sorrowful, even unto death."
Matthew 26:38 (KJV)

"For the joy set before him he endured the cross, scorning its
shame, and sat down at the right hand of the throne of God."
Hebrews 12:2 (NIV)

"And being found in appearance as a man, he humbled him-
self by becoming obedient to death—even death on a cross!"
Philippians 2:8 (NIV)

In Jesus' life's race here on Earth, the cross was the final lap. Everything had been pointing to this moment. He'd done great things—healing, feeding, and raising from the dead—but as He hung on the cross, it was not these worldly achievements that He looked to.

In this moment, in His suffering, He looked ahead, He looked forward, and He looked upward. What He saw gave Him hope; in those final moments, it brought Him the strength he needed.

"Whoever wants to be first among you must be your slave. That is what the Son of Man has done: He came to serve, not be served—and then to give away his life in exchange for the many who are held hostage." Matthew 20:28 (The Message)

Jesus gave His life in exchange for ours. Looking right through the cross to the joy on the other side, Jesus knew His mission and purpose in life.

He followed His mission, not being diverted from His purposes by what those around Him thought. He was faithful in pursuing and fulfilling it, in spite of the personal cost. Neither the scribes and Pharisees nor his family, not even His disciples, could distract Him from pursuing with utter single-mindedness His purpose here on earth.

What was that purpose? The purchase of our freedom, our liberty, and the joy of setting us free.

Following and obeying His Father's perfect will, joy erupted in Heaven as this final task was completed. The triumph as the power of the gates of hell were torn down and defeated, once for all time. A soon return to His heavenly home to be with the Father, surrounded by the glorious sound of angels worshipping at the throne. An unleashing and empowering of millions of followers who would bring His kingdom here on the earth.

As we watch Jesus in the hours leading to the cross at the Mount of Olives, we see Him falling down, crying out to the Father, and wrestling with what He knows is His purpose. He feels that He's being swallowed up by a deep sorrow.

Yet out of that struggle, He returns resolved, purpose fixed, ready to face a painful death. All this for "the joy set before Him". He delays that which is owing to Him as the Son of God in order to fulfil His Father's will. We know that He's counted the cost and made His choice to continue the path to the cross.

John 15:10 tells us to "keep my commandments...abide in my love .... That my joy might remain in you." We can discover the joy of the Lord through following Him, in becoming obedient to His Word, and in spending time with and losing ourselves in Him.

Such is the power of purpose, of obedience, of joy.

Such is the power of being loved and chosen by a perfect Father.

Reflection

Father, thank you that you went to the cross to bring me freedom. Thank you that I am part of the rich inheritance that you purchased at the cross. Thank you for looking at the joy ahead of you rather than the present pain and shame.

Father, I want to unleash your joy in my life. I choose to follow You and to obey you; please help me and strengthen me. I want to know the power of the Holy Spirit working and active in my life.

When I don't understand those bigger purposes of all that is happening in my life, I trust you, knowing that you have a purpose and plan for me. Help me to follow your calling, to share in building your Kingdom here on Earth.

Help me to be faithful in my journey, and continue to strengthen and equip me for all that you have called me to.

Knowing that the Father and the glory of heaven awaits me, let me live my life with that joy in my heart and mind today.

CHAPTER NINE

All of You Will Be Made to Stumble

"All of you will be made to stumble" Matthew 26:31 (WEB)

"Peter replied, 'Even if all fall away on account of you, I never will.' 'Truly I tell you,' Jesus answered, 'this very night, before the rooster crows, you will disown me three times.' But Peter declared, 'Even if I have to die with you, I will never disown you.' And all the other disciples said the same." Matthew 26:33–35 (NIV)

"Those standing there went up to Peter and said, 'Surely you are one of them; your accent gives you away.'

Then he began to call down curses, and he swore to them, 'I don't know the man!'

Immediately a rooster crowed. Then Peter remembered the word Jesus had spoken: 'Before the rooster crows, you will disown me three times.' And he went outside and wept bitterly." Matthew 26:73–75 (NIV)

Jesus warned his friends, the disciples, that they would stumble. Yet His love and friendship for them was undiminished.

Jesus spoke to Peter of his imminent failure, yet He spoke in love. In telling Peter that before the rooster crowed he would deny Him three times, He doesn't condemn him.

Later, His words would bring Peter release and power. Release as he grasped the extent of Jesus' love—that He loves him even though Peter abandoned Him. Power as he realised that despite his weakness and failings, he was still loved and chosen by Jesus.

Ever after, the rooster crowing served as a daily reminder to Peter of his denial. Each time he was faced with a choice, he could remember his failing, or he could choose to remember that his strength was through another. He must put his hope in Jesus and the power of the Holy Spirit alone working in his life.

Every morning as the cock crowed Peter was reminded of putting too much trust in his own strength and had the opportunity to place his trust in the One who could strengthen and empower.

Peter's story of failure to stand by Jesus despite his earlier protestations is one that we remember. Peter, the strong, would reveal his weakness. Known for his rash courage, he would turn away in fear. In these moments, he embodied the opposite of what he would become known for.

"A young man, wearing nothing but a linen garment, was following Jesus. When they seized him, he fled naked, leaving his garment behind." Mark 14:50–52 (NIV)

After Jesus' arrest, another disciple, afraid for his life, fled from the Garden of Gethsemane naked.

We read of two disciples who failed Jesus at this most crucial time. Yet Jesus said that all of the disciples would stumble. We don't know each individual story. It's enough to know that in some way, each of them failed Jesus.

His followers, among them rugged and strong fisherman, had faced and overcome so many challenges. Yet each had to discover that even after spending three years with Jesus, they were still just made of clay.

As they were overwhelmed with shame, they realised their frailness, fallenness, and humanity. The pain of deserting their beloved friend and master made them only more aware of their deep need of His constant companionship.

Each of them had to find a way to live with that failing and move on from this moment. To pick themselves up and start again. Overcome the humiliation and the pain to be all that Jesus called them to be.

So it is with us. As we look around us, we may not know each story, but we know that each one of us is in need of a Saviour. Each one needs the constant support of the One who can lift us up and give us the strength to start again when we fall.

What we learn from the disciples' failure is that Jesus knows us perfectly. He knows us fully. He knows our weaknesses and failings. He knows that we, too, will stumble, that He'll be there to pick us up and set us on the path once more. Our failures no longer define us, for our identity is in Christ.

It may not be a rooster crowing that reminds of us past sins and failings, but there are times we may all be tempted to look backwards, rather than forward; inwards, rather than upward.

We know that in following His leading, we can stay humble, knowing that it is Him working through us rather than anything in and of ourselves.

As we live, in His strength and power, we can follow His plans for our lives and work out their eternal purpose. We can make a daily choice to rely on the power of Jesus through the Holy Spirit working in our lives rather than on our own strength.

Reflection

Father, thank you for this story that helps me see Jesus' disciples in an honest light.

Thank you that you know me fully. Thank you that you know every weakness and failing yet still love me. You know when I will stumble and fall and when I will deny you in word, action, or deed. Thank you that you still love me even as I deny you.

Help me to know you better, and strengthen me by your Holy Spirit.
I choose to follow You.

When I fail you, let me not be discouraged but to remember that like Peter, I am still loved and chosen by You.

CHAPTER TEN

Crucify Him!

As soon as the chief priests and their officials saw him, they shouted,
"Crucify! Crucify!" John 19:6 (NIV)

"Here is your king," Pilate said to the Jews.
But they shouted, "Take him away! Take him away! Crucify him!"
"Shall I crucify your king?" Pilate asked.
"We have no king but Caesar," the chief priests answered.
Finally Pilate handed him over to them to be crucified.
John 19:14-16 (NIV)

Passover was a celebration, a week for the Jewish people to celebrate God releasing them from 400 years of cruel bondage in Egypt.

The Passover reminded them of the time when Moses faced Pharaoh and demanded that the Israelite nation be set free.

Following the terror of ten plagues, the final plague was the death of the firstborn. Each Israelite family was required to slaughter a lamb and daub the blood on their doorposts. In this way, during the night, the angel of death would pass over their homes, and all the firstborn children and animals in their home would be saved.

It was this final plague, striking down Pharaoh's firstborn, that made him relinquish his iron grip and allow the slaves their freedom. He was so crushed by his despair that he agreed that as the nation left, they should be given gifts to take on their journey.

After four hundred years of seemingly unending torment and slavery, the nation was finally set free. God decreed that this night when the angel of death passed over their homes should be remembered every year to remind them of what He had done for them.

If ever there was a feast when freedom should have been uppermost in their minds, it was Passover. If there was ever a time when grace should have been evident in their lives, it was this week.

Jesus came during Passover as the perfect lamb. His blood was shed, just as the lambs', so the people wouldn't suffer the consequences of their sins.

As Jesus arrived in Jerusalem, He was welcomed with palm branches and 'Hosannas', the true Passover spirit. The people shouted out, "Blessed is he who comes in the name of the Lord" (Matthew 23:39 NIV). Those that had travelled up to Jerusalem to celebrate the Passover were in holiday spirit, lining the road with their branches and loud cheers.

Yet in the coming days, whispers started. The scribes and Pharisees, feeling threatened by Him, schemed and plotted.

Wanting to get rid of Jesus, they stirred up whispers about his seemingly illegitimate birth, about this poor Galilean carpenter with the country accent, who wouldn't amount to much.

These powerful men were instrumental in stirring up doubts about Jesus' claims to be the Messiah. In doing so, they dismiss the very One they had been told to anticipate and eagerly expect.

Just a few days after they celebrated Jesus' entering Jerusalem, the nation celebrated the Passover. They remembered a lamb slain for them; they remembered the angel of death passing over their homes, the joy of leaving Egypt as free men and women, set free by God.

What a time of rejoicing this should have been—a time of remembering what a privilege it was to be a part of God's chosen people, to rejoice in being led by Him, chosen by Him, and set free by Him.

Yet they crucified Jesus, the Son of God, during the Passover. Jesus, the lamb of God, was put to death on a cross.

Wherever He turned, Jesus came up against betrayal, criticism, and hate.

Judas, Jesus' disciple and friend, betrayed Him.

The Jewish leaders, who were waiting and looking for the Messiah, sentenced Him to the cruelest death at the hands of the Romans.

The crowds' cheers turned to jeers. Their cries of "Hosanna!" became shouts of "Crucify Him!" Impossibly, they condemned their Messiah to the worst possible beating at the hands of the occupying forces.

Pilate, with the might of the Roman Empire behind him, whilst believing Jesus to be innocent, to appease and calm the angry crowd, sentenced Him to death.

The soldiers charged with His care humiliated and beat him mercilessly, then brutally nailed Him to a cross to die the most painful death of all.

A catalogue of human failings.

Avarice. Jealousy. Hate. Fear.

Forsaken.
Jesus is alone.

Reflection

Father, there but for your grace go I. I've failed you, and I'll fail you again.

Let me always remember my feet of clay.

Help me remember today the freedom that you bought for me. I know it's nothing that I do or have done that makes me acceptable to You.

Thank you for Jesus, who came to be the Passover Lamb who died so that I could be set free.

Empower me with your love and grace to be salt and light to those around me.

Never let me forget the freedom you bought for me that day on the cross. Never let me forget that it was all you and none of me. Never let me forget that I am a forgiven sinner, gloriously set free.

CHAPTER ELEVEN

Spat On & Beaten

"Then some began to spit on Him, and to blindfold Him, and to beat Him, and to say to Him, 'Prophesy!' And the officers struck Him with the palms of their hands." Mark 14:65 (NKJV)

Throughout all that happened to Him, Jesus was still fully in control. Even in the moments when He was being spat on, blindfolded, and beaten, despite appearances, He was in control.

Beating and striking Him seemed to give them power over Him. Despite all that happened to Him, Jesus lost none of His power.

They blindfolded Him perhaps so that they could not see His face, perhaps feeling it would somehow rob Him of His power. To stop His eyes, looking at them with love...so lost in their sinfulness.

Yet whilst these men could cover and silence His eyes that spoke more than a thousand words, they could not silence Him. They could not take away His power, diminish His love, or weaken His resolve. Sinful men delivered undeserved punishment on the only sinless One. Jesus, the One who will declare judgement on us all, was spat on, blindfolded, and beaten.

This beating was orchestrated by frustrated, angry, and outraged religious leaders; agreed to by Pilate; and overseen by his officers. The soldiers who delivered the blows neither knew Him nor had reason to hate Him, yet they unleashed their pent-up anger and hatred on this innocent man.

Every detail of this painful time was later relayed by a witness, as if it was etched in their memory for all eternity. Perhaps someone watching on saw something different in this man. Realising the cruel part they had played in the condemning of an innocent man and His crucifixion, maybe they put their faith in Jesus.

It's all too easy to choose to forget all that Jesus suffered in those painful hours leading up to the crucifixion. He was treated cruelly, misrepresented, and misunderstood. Though undeserving, He suffered cruelly. Jesus was accused, misused and abused, beaten and bruised.

This King of Kings faced His tormenters with humility and love. Fully God, He immersed himself in the cesspit of humanity, the worst of human suffering, so that in every way He can identify with us. The Saviour of the world, in His humanity, embraced physical pain in its worst form.

He became one with us so that we can become one with the Father.

Reflection

Father, thank you for Jesus. Thank you that He bore the blows, was spat on and blindfold for me. He was treated cruelly so that I would not receive your anger. He was spat on, yet I have been raised with Christ. He was blindfold so that I might have the scales fall from my eyes and see the truth of your love for me.

Thank you that whatever I'm facing, you understand...really understand.

You faced it all in those hours before the cross.

CHAPTER TWELVE

The Trial Before Pilate

"He knew that the chief priests had handed Him over because of envy."
Mark 15:10 (NKJV)

"And Pilate, when he had called together the chief priests and the rulers and the people, Said unto them, Ye have brought this man unto me ... I, having examined him before you, have found no fault in this man..."
Luke 23:13–14 (KJV)

"'You have a custom that I release someone for you at the Passover; do you wish then that I release for you the King of the Jews?' So they cried out again, saying, 'Not this Man, but Barabbas.' Now Barabbas was a robber." John 18:39–40 (NIV)

"Pilate had a notice prepared and fastened to the cross. It read: Jesus of Nazareth, the King of the Jews. Many of the Jews read this sign, for the place where Jesus was crucified was near the city, and the sign was written in Aramaic, Latin and Greek. The chief priests of the Jews protested to Pilate, 'Do not write "The King of the Jews," but that this man claimed to be king of the Jews.'
Pilate answered, 'What I have written, I have written.'"
John 19:19-22 (NIV)

Unprecedented events in history continued to unfold.

Just after dawn, Jesus was taken to the governor's palace in Jerusalem to stand trial before Pilate.

It was a clash of powers. The Jews hated the Roman interlopers but were subject to them. Stripped of any real power, they had to defer to Pilate, the Roman governor.

There was no love lost between Pilate and the Jewish leaders. More than once they had humiliated him during his time as ruler. His breeding, birth, and appointment by the Roman emperor carried little weight here in Judea, a backwater of the Roman Empire.

It was early in the morning when Jesus was brought before Pilate for an official trial. Pilate was immediately suspicious. Realising that the Jews had met during the night, he knew they brought Jesus to him with their own agenda. He could see that this man standing before him had stirred up immense hate and envy in their hearts.

There were formal proceedings to follow. Roman trials were much like our own, with both sides speaking, an accusal and a defence. Finally, after hearing the evidence, Pilate would be required to make his decision.

Jesus stood accused "of many crimes" (Mark 15:3, NLT). These alleged crimes included stirring up rebellion, opposing payment of taxes to Caesar, and claiming to be the Christ, the King of the Jews.

The Jewish leaders made their accusations and hoped that Pilate would have no choice but to find Him guilty.

When Pilate questioned Jesus, only on a handful of occasions did Jesus respond. Even then, it was not to defend himself but to speak truth into Pilate's life and to those present.

Pilate was accustomed to those accused before him pleading, begging, and arguing for their freedom and their lives. Never before had he seen the accused respond with silence and with such dignity.

Jesus—beaten, bruised, and battered—was calm and courageous. Despite his pitiful physical state, this man standing in front of Pilate had a strength of purpose he'd never seen before.

His calm peace was a sharp contrast to the outrage and cries of the Jewish leaders.

The quiet dignity of this King of the Jews was far beyond anything that Pilate had ever witnessed.

Pilate's unexpected response was to marvel (Mark 15:5 WEB). This hardened Roman ruler, known for his brutality, was left amazed and wondering by this Galilean carpenter.

Now the chief priests played their ace card. Jesus had called himself a king. Every Jew and Roman citizen knew that laying claim to being king was the one thing that Caesar would not tolerate.

The chief priests thought that they had neatly closed the trap and that the fate of Jesus, this charlatan and usurper, was sealed. Sealed it was—but not by their hand. It was sealed at the dawn of time, the creation of the earth, by the free choice and love of Jesus and His Father.

Pilate, aware of their manipulative plan, shrewdly saw a way around this seemingly impossible situation. Finding no fault in Jesus, he proposed to the gathered crowd that as part of the Passover celebrations, He should be set free.

This Roman invader seemed to grasp the meaning of the Passover better than the religious leaders, understanding that it is about undeserved freedom and being set free.

At this point, there seemed a glimmer of hope that every-thing could be turned around. It seemed that he had found a way out of the neat trap set for him by the religious leaders.

We can almost see his inner struggle. Accustomed to power, used to being surrounded by royalty, Pilate faced this quiet King of the Jews. At several points in the story, we feel that right and truth will prevail and that Pilate will use his power to free Jesus.

In an unprecedented turn of events, this hated Roman ruler, was set against the religious leaders to release this innocent man, this self-proclaimed King who stood accused before him.

As Pilate made his offer to free either Jesus or Barabbas, the religious leaders had an opportunity, a chance to change their minds and release Jesus.

Yet they missed it, instead stirring up the crowd, they encouraging them to release Barabbas to them rather than Jesus. Faced with the choice of following their religious leaders or Pilate, the despised Roman ruler, the crowd sided with the Jewish leaders, crying, "Crucify Him!"

Three times Pilate asked the crowd what he should do with the one they called King of the Jews. Each time the crowd called out more loudly, "Crucify Him!" Trouble was stirring in the crowd. A riot seemed imminent.

Faced with a riot on his hands, Pilate reluctantly made his choice. He acquiesced to the crowd's request, pardoned and released Barabbas, and sentenced Jesus to scourging and crucifixion.

In sight of the crowd, Pilate washed his hands, signifying that he refused to take any responsibility for Jesus' death. Powerless, he realised that he had merely been a tool in the hands of the Jewish leaders.

With such pressure from religious leaders and the crowd, it may feel like Pilate had no choice in the decision he made. Yet we read these words that tell us otherwise: "Pilate, wanting to gratify the crowd..." (Mark 15:15, NKJV). Finally, the truth behind his decision—Pilate feared man more than he feared God.

Pilate believed that Jesus was innocent. Yet with all the power of the Roman Empire at his disposal, he capitulated to the crowd. Despite his inner struggle and unanswered questions, he sentenced this gentle carpenter to be nailed to a wooden cross.

As his final act of power and defiance, Pilate ordered that a sign saying "Jesus of Nazareth, the King of the Jews" be fastened to Jesus' cross. Despite the protests of the chief priests, the sign remained in place. "What I have written, I have written" declared Pilate.

We see unprecedented moments in this story. Pilate, known for his oppression, declared Jesus' innocence.

This governor and member of the aristocracy sided with the poor man from Galilee. Fighting the religious leaders, he looked for a way to release Jesus. This man with much blood on his hands ceremoniously washed his hands of this innocent man's blood. Jesus, the accused, stood silent while Pilate pleaded with him to speak. The Jews clamoured for the Roman overseer to cruelly put to death one of their own people.

As Pilate sought the truth about Jesus, we experience the possibility of hope set against moments of despair and darkness. We see the best of humanity set against the worst. We witness the powerful humbled and the humble holding ultimate power.

Reflection

Father, thank you for Jesus. Father, I want to be amazed and astonished by Jesus, by His love, and by His compassion and love. Please open my heart to understand the depth of all that Jesus did for me. Help me to walk in His strength and compassion.

Holy Spirit, help me to be calm and courageous when I face those who accuse me. Today I make my choice to place my trust in You.

CHAPTER THIRTEEN

A Son of the Father – What's in a Name?

"And they had then a notorious prisoner called Barabbas."
Matthew 27:16 (ESV)

"So when the crowd had gathered, Pilate asked them, 'Which one do you want me to release to you: Jesus Barabbas, or Jesus who is called the Messiah?'" Matthew 27:17 (NIV)

"'What shall I do, then, with Jesus who is called the Messiah?' Pilate asked. They all answered, 'Crucify him!'" Matthew 27:22 (NIV)

When Judas led the chief priests, the officers of the temple guard, and the elders to where Jesus was praying in the Garden of Gethsemane, Jesus' response was "Am I leading a rebellion, that you have come with swords and clubs?"

Perhaps He was referring to Barabbas, a notorious revolutionary, who had incited a riot and who had indeed been arrested for his part in a rebellion. Jesus was a man on a mission, who had come in peace. Both men had been sentenced to death by the authorities. Both had the opportunity of a reprieve from the Jewish people as part of the traditional Passover festivities, a goodwill gesture.

These two men had more in common than it would at first appear. The name Barabbas means 'son of the father'. Both men had an opportunity to be freed as part of the Passover tradition. One, Barabbas, the son of an earthly father. The other, Jesus, the son of His heavenly Father.

One sinful, one sinless.
One rebellious, one obedient.
One notorious, one a barely-known carpenter from Nazareth.
One fallen, one pure and holy.

Throughout Jesus' trial, Pilate avoided using His name, Jesus, the name with which we are so familiar. Instead, he addressed him as 'King of the Jews' and 'Messiah', strange names indeed to refer to the accused. It seems incredible that it was the Roman judge who was used to remind both Jesus and the Jews of His true name and identity as the Messiah.

It's almost as if Pilate was reminding the people that this man could be their Messiah, that they were making a conscious choice to reject Him. What was clear to Pilate was missed by those who were waiting for their Messiah. It's no wonder that watching this travesty of justice, Pilate chose to wash his hands of the whole sorry affair.

When Pilate asked them, who do you want me to release to you, the power of his words was lost in translation.

He was asking them which son of the father he should release to them. Which son?

Barabbas, the guilty son of an earthly father is set free, while Jesus, the innocent son of the Heavenly Father was condemned.

Reflection

Father, thank you for Jesus, your precious Son.

Thank you that He was condemned that I might be set free.

Thank you that you reveal yourself to those whom you choose.

Thank you that I can come to know you through your son Jesus.

CHAPTER FOURTEEN

What Jesus Faced at the Cross

"He holds his priesthood permanently, because he continues forever. Consequently, he is able to save to the uttermost those who draw near to God through him, since he always lives to make intercession for them."
Hebrews 7:24–25 (ESV)

"And being in an agony he prayed more earnestly; and his sweat became like great drops of blood falling down to the ground."
Luke 22:44 (ESV)

"In all their affliction, he was afflicted," Isaiah 63:9 (ESV)

Jesus was praying alone in the Garden of Gethsemane. As He prayed, He sweated, the stress so great that His sweat was like drops of blood.

If we ever wonder whether Jesus understood what would happen in the coming hours, we only need to look back at His struggle in the Garden to realise that He completely understood it, all that He faced.

As He knelt in the garden, He knew everything that was about to happen, He stood firm to the choice made at the very beginning of creation to come to save a people for Himself.

This course was set for Him from the beginning of time itself. The Son of God, knowing Who He is, stepped down from heaven. Surrounded by the worshipping angels, he was born into the vulnerability of a manger in a stable. Just a few years later, Jesus stood in a garden awaiting the moment of betrayal, once again vulnerable.

What He faced in the next few hours would be enough to crush any man—shame, dishonour, ridicule, rejection, abandonment, loneliness, temptation, misunderstanding, physical pain, and death.

He was accused and disowned by His own people.

He was ridiculed by the Roman soldiers, invaders of a land belonging to and inhabited by His people.

He faced rejection by the very people for whom He had come as Messiah.

He was abandoned by those He was saving and by his close friends.

He was alone. Not only abandoned by his friends and family, but He was apart from His Father for the first time in history.

He was tempted to forgo this painful path that had been planned for all eternity.

He was misunderstood. Even those close to Him, whom He had shared his days with, didn't seem to comprehend who He was and what He was facing.

He experienced pain, excruciating pain. He was beaten, scourged, hungry, exhausted. The scourging alone was enough to kill many ordinary men. The final agony—the most painful death the Romans could conceive—crucifixion on a wooden cross. A long, slow death. Struggling for breath. Pain wracking his bruised and beaten body.

Finally, death. The ultimate victory.

In His final hours, He experienced every kind of suffering. Nothing was held back. He endured suffering to its fullest degree.

In all this, the hardest thing to bear was not the pain, nor the abandonment, but our sin. As He completely identified with us in every way by taking on our sins, God's anger was poured out on Him. This was the cup that He drank—the cup of God's wrath. Jesus drank the cup that should have been ours, right down to the last drop. He left nothing undone.

As He took on the sins of mankind, He endured the agony of separation from His Father.

Crying, "It is finished," He could finally let go. He had done it all. He had walked the path for us and won the victory over sin. His mission was completed. Finished.

Did Jesus understand what faced Him? Yes, absolutely.

He went through every imaginable type of suffering. He understood all that was needed to save us and willingly went through it because of His love for us. We can never say that He doesn't understand.

Jesus understood fully yet loved you and me enough to walk the path to the cross.

If ever we should stand in amazement, it is as we realise the fullness of the beauty and majesty of this mighty Saviour. This Saviour... magnificent as He wrestled with His destiny in a lonely garden.

If we ever wonder if Jesus understands what we are facing today, the rejection, pain, temptation and loneliness, the answer is a resounding YES!

Reflection

Father, thank you that Jesus knew everything. He knew all that He faced yet willingly suffered in every way.

Thank you that Jesus identified Himself with suffering and pain. Thank you that You understand my sufferings and challenges.

As I reflect on Jesus' last hours before His death, help me to be in awe and amazement of that reality of all that Jesus went through, just for me. Let it lead me to worship and praise of your name.

CHAPTER FIFTEEN

The Disciples' Response

"For it is written, 'I will strike the shepherd, and the sheep of the flock will be scattered.'"
Matthew 26:31 (ESV), referencing Zechariah 13:7

"Behold, the time ... has now come, that you will be scattered ."
John 16:32 (WEB)

"And they all left him and fled."
Mark 14:50 (ESV)

D evastated.

Afraid.
Weak.
Fearful.
Denial.

These words describe the response of the disciples as Jesus was arrested and taken from them, the reactions of those who were closest to Jesus as He was put on trial and faced the cross.

These same disciples had asked for the "highest places of honour in your glory" (Mark 10:37, MSG), had left everything to follow Him, had heard Jesus talk about "taking up their cross", and were happy to be identified with Christ as He reached out to heal.

Yet as Judas arrived to betray Jesus under the cover of darkness, accompanied by men with clubs and swords, these men ran. At the moment when Jesus most needed the support of His friends, they fled into the night.

During the agonising hours that followed, the disciples were conspicuous by their absence. Only Peter and John were seen watching what happened to Jesus. They waited in the courts of the high priest as He faced his trial. John stood looking on as Jesus hung dying on the cross.

After sharing Jesus' life every single day for many months, those most identified with Him disappeared into the city and the hills.

As Jesus spent the next few hours alone, so too did His disciples. They experienced their own anguish and agony, fearful of man and ashamed of deserting their beloved friend, rabbi, and master.

Finally, after Jesus' death and resurrection, the disciples re-assembled, with the "doors locked for fear of the Jews". (John 20:19 HCSB®)

It is to these unlikely and undeserving men that the resurrected Jesus came. He came to show His love and to reveal the final step in the eternal plan for the redemption of man.

Yet Jesus foreknew their desertion, fear, and denial...He knew everything. From the beginning, He knew.

He knew...as He walked along the shores of the Sea of Galilee, seeing Simon and Andrew, James and John, and calling, "Follow Me ... I will make you fish for people!" (Mark 1:17, HCSB®)

He knew...as He sent them out two by two with authority over unclean spirits (Mark 6:7, ESV).

He knew...as He patiently taught them and opened up the Scriptures to them, that they would forget and flee.

He knew...as they walk towards Jerusalem and He told them all that would happen to Him, that in the heat and fear of the moment, they would abandon Him.

He knew...as He knelt before each of the twelve disciples and washed their feet, that they would scatter in the face of His hardest trial.

Jesus was not ignorant of who they were. He knew each fault, weakness, and failing of each disciple...and still, He chose each one of them—even Judas, the one who would betray Him and hand Him over to the Jewish leaders.

During those painful hours, reeling from the betrayal, waiting and watching, the disciples learnt something that they would never forget. Strong as it was, their love for Jesus wasn't enough to stop them from running. Their passionate devotion and commitment to Him was insufficient to fight their fear. They realised that they were unequal to the task that Jesus had so clearly laid out for them.

Their brokenness, however, was the very pathway to power. Their knowledge of their weakness, the doorway to strength. No longer would they trust in their own abilities, reasoning, or courage. Instead, they would learn to rely on the empowering One that Jesus sent to them: the Comforter, the Holy Spirit.

Finally, they understood the extent of Jesus' love for them. A love that conquers fear. A love that perseveres, hopes, and trusts. A love that isn't determined by their actions but is defined by its own rules. Heavenly rules. A love that loves and welcomes the fearful, unlovely, and weak.

It was this love and power that went to the cross and to the grave, rose again, appeared to the disciples, and, true to its promise, sent the Holy Spirit to strengthen and comfort them. It was this same love that accepted them as they were, but wanted them to become so much more.

This same love that enabled weak disciples to triumph, fearful disciples to overcome, running disciples to stand firm and fight.

It was His love that transformed a bunch of cowards into men who faced their fears, changed the world and stood firm to the last.

Reflection

Father, thank you that the disciples were just ordinary men chosen by you.

Thank you that you loved them even though you knew that they would betray and disappoint you. Thank you for the hope this brings. Thank you that you love me...whatever. Thank you that your love is not dependent on my ability, actions, or faith.

Thank you that you can use me in spite of my weaknesses and failings.

Thank you that you love me and chose me. Help me today to walk the path you have chosen for me with love and patience.

CHAPTER SIXTEEN

It's Friday, but Sunday's Coming

"'You who are going to destroy the temple and build it in three days, save yourself! Come down from the cross, if you are the Son of God!' In the same way the chief priests, the teachers of the law and the elders mocked him. 'He saved others,' they said, 'but he can't save himself!'"
Matthew 27:40–42 (NIV)

"I lay down My life so that I may take it again. No one has taken it away from Me, but I lay it down on My own initiative. I have authority to lay it down, and I have authority to take it up again."
John 10:17–18 (NASB)

"I looked again, and I heard the voices of thousands and millions of angels around the throne and of the living beings and the elders. And they sang in a mighty chorus:

'Worthy is the Lamb who was slaughtered—
to receive power and riches
and wisdom and strength
and honour and glory and blessing.'"
Revelation 5:12 (NLT)

At any point in His life, Jesus could have cried for help from His Father. Thousands of angels awaited His call.

Jesus had come from Heaven, where He was surrounded by thousands upon thousands of worshipping angels.

When He stood, seemingly alone in the Garden of Gethsemane, the angels were still waiting.

Jesus stood there, knowing who He is and who the Father is. He knew that He had only to ask and the Father would send thousands of angels instantly.

He himself made this point as His accusers came to arrest Him in the Garden of Gethsemane.

"Don't you realize that I could ask my Father for thousands of angels to protect us, and he would send them instantly?"
Matthew 26:53 (NLT)

He knew that no man could hold Him, except by the Father's express permission. No hand could hit him, except by the Father's divine purpose. No nail could pierce His body, except with the Father's foreknowledge and approval.

At every point of His journey towards the cross, He could have called out to His Father. He could have cried out for the Father to save Him and send the angels. Thousands upon thousands of angels!

At each point of His journey, the Father could have swept down from Heaven to take Him home.

Yet Jesus chose to go to the cross. With each step, with each breath He took, Jesus knew exactly who He was and is. He knew

EXPERIENCE EASTER | 85

that the Father could rescue Him. He knew the divine plan whispered before all creation.

As He was accused by the religious leaders, sentenced by Pilate, and beaten by the Roman soldiers, He was fully conscious of His Sonship.

As He faced the mocking worship of the soldiers, was scourged, and was led to the cross, He knew that He would shortly sit as their judge.

As the nails were driven into the rough wooden beam of the cross, Jesus knew He was the precious Son of the Father.

As He was mocked by the criminals on either side of Him, as insults were hurled by passersby, He knew He was loved by the Father.

He knew that He was the Son of Man, that the power that they seemed to have over Him had an expiry date—in just three days He would be sitting at the right hand of power. It was Friday, but He knew that Sunday was coming!

As He endured those final painful hours of the long-lingering, agonising death, with each painful breath, He chose not to call on the angels. He chose instead to love, to surrender, and to obey. He chose death—death that brings life.

Knowing that it was His eternal destiny to have thousands upon thousands of angels worship Him, declaring Him to be the only One who is worthy, He waited, knowing that His time would come and that the wait would be worth it all.

Maybe it was this final journey of Christ that Paul was thinking of when he wrote to the Ephesians, "I pray that you...may...grasp how wide and long and high and deep is the love of Christ" Ephesians 3:17–18 (NIV).

Each step, each choice in those final hours, demonstrates so clearly the width, length, height, and depth of His love for us.

Reflection

Father, thank you that you sent Jesus. Thank you that each step He took towards the cross was His choice to show how much I am loved.

Father, help me to understand the depths of your love for me...the love that sent your Son to such a painful death...the love that calls me also to love, surrender, and obey.

Father, sometimes I feel so weak. Please fill me with your Holy Spirit today. Empower me to walk in surrender and obedience to you. Help me with the choices that I face today to make decisions that will bring glory to your name.

CHAPTER SEVENTEEN

The Thief and
the Carpenter

"And with him they crucified two robbers, one on his right and one on his left." Mark 15:27 (ESV)

"So also the chief priests, with the scribes and elders, mocked him, saying, 'He saved others; he cannot save himself. He is the King of Israel; let him come down now from the cross, and we will believe in him. He trusts in God; let God deliver him now, if he desires him. For he said, "I am the Son of God."' And the robbers who were crucified with him also reviled him in the same way." Matthew 27:41–44 (ESV)

"One of the criminals who were hanged railed at him, saying, 'Are you not the Christ? Save yourself and us!' But the other rebuked him, saying, 'Do you not fear God, since you are under the same sentence of condemnation? And we indeed justly, for we are receiving the due reward of our deeds; but this man has done nothing wrong.' And he said, 'Jesus, remember me when you come into your kingdom.' And he said to him, 'Truly, I say to you, today you will be with me in Paradise.'"
Luke 23:39–43 (ESV)

Jesus, the perfect Son, was crucified. On either side of Him hung two robbers.

One thief cursed Jesus, his savage criticism mirroring that of the Jewish leaders who stood around mocking Him.

"He saved others ... yet He cannot save Himself!" he cried.

"He is the King of Israel; let Him now come down from the cross, and we will believe in Him." Matthew 27:42 (ESV)

"He trusts in God. Let God rescue him now if he wants him, for he said, 'I am the Son of God.'" Matthew 27:43 (NIV)

This thief raged against Jesus even as he himself hung dying on a cross.

Just a few hours later, the other thief had been changed completely by witnessing Jesus as He suffered on the cross.

In response to the abusive words of one thief, who challenged Jesus, "Are you not the Christ? Save yourself and us!" (Luke 23:39, ESV), his fellow thief responded, "Have you no fear of God? You're getting the same as him. We deserve this, but not him—he did nothing to deserve this" (Luke 23:41- The Message).

Turning to Jesus, this man, broken by hour after hour of agonising pain, asked Him, "Jesus, remember me when you come into your kingdom!" Luke 23:42, (ESV).

Within hours of meeting Jesus, this thief acknowledged that he was suffering the consequences of his own sins and asked Jesus very simply to save him. This cursing, blaming thief was changed by the unchanging One who hung silently on the cross next to his.

Something about Jesus, even as death approached, drew men to Himself and provoked them to turn to God.

Even as He hung on the cross, in His humanity, Jesus showed us the Father in all His glory.

Unchanging – The hours on the cross did not change Jesus as they did the angry thief. He was still fixed on His purpose, the saving of mankind, the sacrifice of a truly innocent man.

Compassionate – Rising on the painful nails, He took one painful breath to bring this thief comfort and hope: "Truly, I say to you, today you shall be with me in Paradise" (Luke 23:43 ESV). He also ensured that His mother was cared for (John 19:26–27). He continued to speak truth to reach those who witnessed His final hours.

Sinless – In all the agony of His crucifixion, He did not sin. In the depths of His suffering, He did not curse, blame or feel hatred for those who had placed Him there.

Forgiving – Not once did He utter words to curse the men at His feet who rebuked and condemned Him. As they crucified Him and cast lots to divide His garments, He spoke only forgiveness: "Father, forgive them, for they know not what they do" Luke 23:34 (ESV). In one breath, He forgave those who had been hurling curses at Him.

Sovereign & Saviour – Even now, He welcomed sinners into Heaven. He came to the cross of His own choice and free will. His spirit was not taken from Him but was willingly given up as He committed His spirit to the Father. He alone had the authority to lay down His life and the authority to take it up again. John 10:17–18 (ESV)

In His darkest hour, facing the toughest trial of all, Jesus did not waver but stood firm. Facing betrayal and persecution, He was unmoving. Nailed to a cross, He was steadfast in purpose. Dying, He was compassionate.

In the shadow of the Cross, we see the Father's person and love perfectly demonstrated in Jesus.

Reflection

Thank you Father that you never change, that you're always trustworthy, always faithful, always there.

Thank you that it's never too late – that I can always come to you – knowing that you love me and will forgive me, however far I've run from you, whatever I've done.

Thank you that your arms are open wide, even on the cross - welcoming me, a sinner, into your loving arms.

CHAPTER EIGHTEEN

Remarkable Life, Extraordinary Death

"At noon, darkness fell across the whole land until three o'clock."
Mark 15:33 (NLT)

"Many holy people who had died were raised to life...they went into the holy city and appeared to many people."
Matthew 27:52–53 (GOD'S WORD)

"Now the centurion, and those who were with him keeping guard over Jesus, when they saw the earthquake and the things that were happening, became very frightened and said, 'Truly this was the Son of God!'" Matthew 27:54 (NASB)

Jesus' extraordinary life leaves us speechless with wonder. His healing and miracles leave us breathless with amazement.

Even in death, Jesus continued to amaze people. His last hours on the earth were filled with the most extraordinary events.

As Jesus hung on the cross, darkness fell. Even though it was the middle of the day, this darkness lasted for three hours, right up until the time of His death. This darkness mirrored the blackness of our sin and the deep sadness in the heart of the Father as He gave up His Son to pay the ultimate price.

As he hung on the cross, Jesus was offered the usual cup of wine mixed with gall to dull the pain and help numb His senses. Jesus refused to take it, choosing to stay fully conscious, fully present during His final hours.

Only a handful of times did He speak. Unlike the criminals on either side of Him, it was neither to curse, insult, nor mock.

As He died, Jesus uttered a loud cry and breathed his last. At this exact moment, the curtain of the temple was torn in two, from top to bottom. This heavy curtain, representing the separation between God and man, the veil between the high priest and the most holy place, was torn, but not by the hands of man.

History records that this curtain was of substantial size and weight, measuring 18 metres high and 100mm thick. Yet the hand of God rent this in two in a moment. The separation between God and man was dealt with through the death of God's Son.

At the same time, Matthew writes of the earth shaking and rocks splitting. Those looking on as Jesus died experienced not only an earthquake but witnessed the very rocks around them breaking apart.

As this happened, tombs were broken open. Later, after Jesus' resurrection, godly men and women were raised to life and appeared to people in Jerusalem.

Whatever phenomena these were, although we may find it hard to understand, the timing is extraordinary. Perfect.

Even in the manner of His death, Jesus drew people to Himself, revealing Himself through His suffering.

The Roman centurion and those guarding Jesus, seeing all that happened, were terrified. They exclaimed "Surely, He was the Son of God!" (Matthew 27:54 NIV). The centurion and the Roman soldiers accompanying him were accustomed to putting people to death by crucifixion, they had probably witnessed many such deaths. Yet none that they had witnessed was like this.

Something about this man, His life and death, was so different as to make them cry out, aware that something astounding was happening before their eyes. These hardened soldiers had never seen anything like this.

When the crowds that gathered to watch the spectacle saw what took place, they returned home "beating their breasts" (Luke 23:48 ESV), an expression for those experiencing heart-felt anguish.

This rough crowd had come together for the questionable pre-Sabbath entertainment and spectacle of watching criminals die by crucifixion. Yet something moved them, so much so that they went home deeply sorrowful.

Through all these happenings and events, it is clear that God was at work. At this crucial and momentous point in history, these events marked the death of Jesus as something quite separate, set apart, and quite extraordinary.

During His life, Jesus was accompanied by signs and wonders. In His death, we see incredible happenings and events.

Jesus' life and death were remarkable. Unprecedented. Extraordinary.

Reflection

Father, thank you for Jesus. Thank you that both His life and death were so remarkable and that His life was so full of wonderful events. Thank you that you gave us these signs to point to Jesus as your Son.

Thank you that you give us the Holy Spirit, that you call me to walk a life filled with your Holy Spirit power.

Father, I long to be filled with your Holy Spirit. I hunger to be continually amazed by Jesus and empowered and by You. Please fill me today with your Holy Spirit so that I might know your power in my life.

CHAPTER NINETEEN

The Forsaken Son

"At noon, darkness came over the whole land until three in the afternoon. And at three in the afternoon Jesus cried out in a loud voice, 'Eloi, Eloi, lema sabachthani?' (which means 'My God, my God, why have you forsaken me?')." Mark 15:33 NIV

"The Lord has laid on Him the iniquity of us all" Isaiah 53:6 NIV

"For him who knew no sin he made to be sin on our behalf; so that in him we might become the righteousness of God."
2 Corinthians 5:21 (WEB)

"But he was pierced for our transgressions. He was crushed for our iniquities. The punishment that brought our peace was on him"
Isaiah 53:5 (WEB)

In the final moments on the cross, Jesus uttered these words:

"My God, my God, why have you forsaken me?"
Psalm 22:1 (NIV)

The darkest moment in history. The Father turned His face away.

Jesus, forsaken by the Father, stood in the place of guilty sinners. Overwhelmed by God's wrath. Crushed by the weight of our sin.

The great exchange took place. Jesus took on our iniquity. In return, He gifted His own righteousness to us.

In the dark days leading up to the cross, Jesus has focused on the joy set before Him. Yet in these moments on the cross, bearing the sin of all mankind seemingly overwhelmed Him. The separation from the Father was unbearable. The darkness complete.

As the Father turned away, unable to look on the sin as it fell on His Son, Jesus drank the bitterest cup of all.

He was forsaken by His Father. All the joy and delight that He found in fellowship with the Father...cut off. The Father's precious presence...gone. The sustaining love of the Father...absent.

At the moment Jesus sacrificed all, the Father looked away. There was no voice from heaven reminding Jesus that He was the beloved son.
Instead...silence...anguish...desolation. Abandoned in His suffering. Alone in death.

Even during these last breaths, Jesus spoke words that point those looking on to His true identity as the suffering Saviour, the One who was to be sent by the Father.

Asking why He had been forsaken, He knew the answer, for this redemption had been planned from the beginning of time. Jesus, being sent, coming as the sin offering for the world, had been the Father's intention for endless ages.

The total abandonment that Jesus faced on the cross ushered in the most amazing promise for us. His separation means that we can never be separated from the Father. The One who forsook His own Son, Jesus, on the cross will never forsake you.

Because Jesus died such a death and took your sins, you can be reconciled to the Father. Jesus' suffering brings you peace. His alienation brings you the offer to become a child of God. His rejection brings you the constant companionship of the Holy Spirit. His death brings you life—in all its fullness.

Instead of knowing alienation, darkness, and distance, He invites you to come closer. To embrace His presence. Know His sustaining love. Enjoy His fellowship.

Reflection

Father, thank you for Jesus. Thank you that He took my sins and died the death that I should die so that I can live and be set free.

Thank you that I can trust you in the most challenging times...yes, even in death. That I can come close to you and know Your presence.

Thank you that whatever happens, you promise never to leave or forsake me.

CHAPTER TWENTY

The Final Honour

"Joseph of Arimathea, a respected member of the council, who was also himself looking for the kingdom of God, took courage and went to Pilate and asked for the body of Jesus." Mark 15:43 (ESV)

"Now Joseph was a disciple of Jesus, but secretly because he feared the Jewish leaders." John 19:38 (NIV)

"As evening approached, there came a rich man from Arimathea, named Joseph, who had himself become a disciple of Jesus." Matthew 27:57 (NIV)

"a man named Joseph, a member of the Council, a good and upright man, who had not consented to their decision and action. He came from the Judean town of Arimathea, and he himself was waiting for the kingdom of God."
Luke 23:50–51 (NIV)

He was accompanied by Nicodemus, the man who earlier had visited Jesus at night. Nicodemus brought a mixture of myrrh and aloes, about seventy-five pounds. Taking Jesus' body, the two of them wrapped it, with the spices, in strips of linen. This was in accordance with Jewish burial customs.
John 19:39–40 (NIV)

Following Jesus' death, and with evening fast approaching, there remained only a few hours to give Him the final honour of burial before the Sabbath.

Yet it was not Peter, John, the disciples, or even Lazarus who had the courage to step forward at this crucial moment in history. It was Joseph of Arimathea, a member of the very council that so recently had condemned Jesus to a brutal death.

As a highly respected and prominent member of the Jewish council, until this moment he had followed Jesus in secret because he feared the Jewish leaders. What he saw and experienced as he stood watching Jesus on the cross changed him forever. He couldn't hide any longer, now filled with great courage.

Realising that the body could not stay on the cross during the Sabbath and needing to move swiftly, Joseph acted. His fears vanished. Knowing what he must do, he braved the wrath of Pilate's temper, risked the outrage and indignation of his fellow council members, and boldly entered the courts of Pilate to ask for Jesus' body. He risked everything, put everything on the line, to honour Jesus.

Pilate's response is surprising. At first, he was amazed that Jesus was already dead as it was not uncommon for criminals to hang on the cross for days before finally expiring. Pilate checked with the centurion overseeing the crucifixion, that Jesus really was dead, then granted Joseph permission to bury the body.

There was some haste, as the body must be laid to rest before the Sabbath commenced at sundown. Honouring and keeping the Sabbath holy would have been important to any Jew but especially so to a religious leader, such as Joseph.

Joseph and Nicodemus took Jesus' body down from the cross and prepared it for burial. Fearful in life, they boldly come to honour Jesus for this final solemn ritual.

In God's perfect timing, Joseph's wealth had purchased and prepared a new tomb, ready as his own final resting place. Little did he know how God had ordained this before the beginning of time to provide a place to lay the broken and mutilated body of His precious Son.

This once-hesitant disciple, now courageous and fearless, gave what he had that was of value to honour the broken body of Jesus. He placed Jesus' body in his own tomb—a generous gift from a humble follower.

He was unaware that the tomb would only be needed by Jesus for a few hours. It was only two days before His resurrection, when the disciples would stand outside the empty tomb astonished and amazed.

Joseph alone had the position of power and authority to ask Pilate for the body. He was the one who had a newly hewn tomb prepared for burial. Overcoming his previous fear of man, he did what he could for Jesus. This man was not remembered for his fear but for his courage and generosity.

As one woman is forever remembered for anointing Jesus' feet so Joseph is remembered for offering Him a place of burial.

Reflection

Father, thank you that even in Jesus' death, you had a perfect plan. Thank you that one man was able to overcome his fears, becoming courageous in what he did for your Son.

In the same way, help me to overcome my own fear of man, of what people will say and think, to follow You.

Help me to be courageous and to be generous, and help me to do what I can for you today.

CHAPTER TWENTY ONE

The Women's Response

"Near the cross of Jesus stood his mother, his mother's sister, Mary the wife of Clopas, and Mary Magdalene." John 19:25 (NIV)

"Some women were watching from a distance. Among them were Mary Magdalene, Mary the mother of James the younger and of Joseph, and Salome. In Galilee these women had followed him and cared for his needs. Many other women who had come up with him to Jerusalem were also there." Mark 15:40–41 (NIV)

"Mary Magdalene and Mary the mother of Joseph saw where he was laid." Mark 15:47 (NIV)

"When the Sabbath was over, Mary Magdalene, Mary the mother of James, and Salome bought spices so that they might go to anoint Jesus' body." Mark 16:1 (NIV)

During those long hours on the cross, the most significant event in all of history, Jesus' devoted women followers were present throughout. It was they who witnessed the quiet agony of His ordeal, this most cruel of executions.

It was women who hastened to the tomb early on Sunday morning to wrap His body with spices and perfumes, faithfully performing this last service for Jesus.

Motivated by love, these women had followed, served, and supported Jesus from Galilee. They had left their homes to come to Jerusalem with Him. As the disciples scattered, these women were drawn together by a common bond of love for the innocent suffering of their beloved Master.

Safe in the knowledge that their faces were not known in the temple courts and to the Jewish leaders who had persecuted Him, unseen and unnoticed, these women followed Jesus, witnessed Him struggling to carry His cross, saw the nails driven into His hands, and watched as the cross was raised above them.

Their dreams in tatters, faithful to the last, all they could do now was to watch this torture of their beloved Master at the hands of Roman executioners.

They stood watching the cross at a distance. As Jesus's agony intensified, it seems they stepped away from the cross, unable to bear watching this cruel suffering and not wanting Him to witness their weeping and grief so close at hand.

Powerless, they watched His crucifixion take place before their eyes—utterly involved and completely present, powerless to ease His suffering, witnesses to His death.

They wept bitter tears as the soldier pierced Jesus' side, proving beyond doubt that no life remained in His body, their beloved master so cruelly taken from them.

Some of the women followed as Joseph and Nicodemus took Jesus' battered body down from the cross, placing it in a tomb close by. They watched as the tomb was sealed with resounding finality, death seemingly triumphant.

Hurrying home for the Sabbath, they spent a day counting the hours until sundown, when they could purchase the spices and perfumes they needed for their Master.

After a sleepless night, they arose before dawn, running without a clear plan to the grave to embalm Jesus' body. Even now they sought to show Him their love, honouring Him in death. They prepared for a burial, not a resurrection and an empty tomb, failing to understand all that Jesus had spoken about himself.

It was to women that the angels spoke of the risen Lord Jesus, to a woman that Jesus revealed himself in the garden, and for women to witness and share the good news that Jesus is alive.

Jesus turned the world on its head, giving these loyal women followers an unprecedented place in history.

Just a few days later, the women were present in the Upper Room, when Peter addressed the gathered "brothers and sisters" (Acts 1:16 NIV) as they waited together for the promised Holy Spirit.

This handful of women, previously invisible, was rewarded with what was most precious to them: the precious presence of Jesus. Empowered by the Spirit. Entrusted with a message to share.

Reflection

Father, we read of women watching as Jesus dies, witnessing an empty tomb, then meeting a resurrected Jesus. Thank you that you have revealed yourself to me, that meeting and following you has changed me forever.

Thank you that although their devotion and actions were often unseen, in Jesus' final hours, we see how special they are to Him.

Thank you that you chose these women for a special role. That like these women, you have given me a heart to love and share with others in difficult times. Help me to love you more, to love your presence, and to depend on your promised Holy Spirit each day as I seek to follow You.

CHAPTER TWENTY TWO

The Final Journey & Burial

"Now when evening had come, because it was... the day before the Sabbath, Joseph of Arimathea, a prominent council member...went in to Pilate and asked for the body of Jesus. Pilate...granted the body to Joseph. Then he bought fine linen, took Him down, and wrapped Him in the linen. And he laid Him in a tomb which had been hewn out of the rock."
Mark 15:42–46 (NKJV)

Nothing could have prepared Jesus' disciples for the cruelty and pain that would be inflicted on their Master prior to His death. Nothing could have prepared anyone for the grim task of taking Jesus' body down from the cross to His place of burial.

In these few words about Joseph of Arimathea, we read of one of the most beautiful acts of worship and honour in the Bible.

One follower, who remained at the foot of the cross, pledged that Jesus would suffer no further indignities. After asking Pilate for the body, Joseph returned to the scene of Jesus' execution.

His grim task: to assist Jesus' final passage to a burial tomb; to honour Him in death.

Jesus' lifeless, broken body was taken down from the cross, the cruel nails removed. His face and body were barely recognisable as the One who knelt in the garden less than twenty-four hours before.

Yet who would have the courage, love, and compassion to touch His body, to hold Him, to carry Him, when to do so would mean defilement and dishonour in the world's eyes?

Into this arena stepped the most unlikely of persons: Joseph, a prominent man and council member, esteemed for his wisdom and holy life. The role he played is extraordinary - Joseph accepted the unlikely privilege of becoming defiled through touching Jesus' dead and bloody body.

His choice would change his life. Yet this man of God threw off everything that might hinder him—his position, wealth, and power—choosing instead a path of humility, love, and sacrifice. A man used to giving orders to others, Joseph could have brought servants or convinced disciples to undertake this daunting task. He could so easily have passed on this gift to another.

Yet it was Joseph himself who took Jesus' body down from the cross, who wrapped His broken body in the best linen and gave Him a place of honour in a newly hewn tomb.

We can't even begin to imagine this task. Ribbons of flesh hung from Jesus's back, blood was caked on His body, a hole was in His side, and His face was bruised and bloodied. How or where could Joseph touch and hold this bruised and bloody body? How did he control his physical reaction to seeing the bones and sinews visible on Jesus' back from the cruel scourging?

His final passage, Jesus was carried across the rough ground, strewn with rocks, to the place of burial.

How moving, this solemn ritual, as Joseph prepared Jesus for His burial. What love, sacrifice, and honour for this esteemed man of Jerusalem to become bloodied and unclean. Fighting back his own feelings, He did all that was necessary to honour this King.

Whilst others looked on, seeing defilement and shame, Joseph saw only blessing and honour.

Unknowing, He was the first one to be touched by the blood of this holy, slain lamb, whom so many more would come to know.

Reflection

Father, once again I am amazed. Joseph, a man who had everything, counted it as nothing when it came to showing love and honour to Jesus.

I am astounded at his choice to give up everything for you.

Help me not to hold on to things of this world, to the privileges that I enjoy, but to follow you wherever you lead me.

Let me be someone who does whatever it takes to follow you.

CHAPTER TWENTY THREE

Glorious Day

"At the crack of dawn on Sunday, the women came to the tomb carrying the burial spices they had prepared. They found the entrance stone rolled back from the tomb, so they walked in. But once inside, they couldn't find the body of the Master Jesus.

They were puzzled, wondering what to make of this. Then, out of nowhere it seemed, two men, light cascading over them, stood there. The women were awestruck and bowed down in worship. The men said, 'Why are you looking for the Living One in a cemetery? He is not here, but raised up. Remember how he told you when you were still back in Galilee that he had to be handed over to sinners, be killed on a cross, and in three days rise up?' Then they remembered Jesus' words."
Luke 24:1–8 (The Message)

"As they entered the tomb, they saw a young man dressed in a white robe sitting on the right side, and they were alarmed.

'Don't be alarmed,' he said. 'You are looking for Jesus the Nazarene, who was crucified. He has risen! He is not here. See the place where they laid him. But go, tell his disciples and Peter, "He is going ahead of you into Galilee. There you will see him, just as he told you."'

Trembling and bewildered, the women went out and fled from the tomb." Mark 16:5–8 NIV

The most glorious day—everything in history had been leading up to this.

It was early—dawn—as the women came to anoint Jesus' body and found the stone rolled away to reveal an empty tomb. The body was gone. The soldiers guarding the tomb absent. The woman were perplexed—this was an unexpected turn of events.

While they were standing, weeping and bewildered, a bright light dazzled them. Before them appeared two men whose very clothing gleamed with light. Afraid, they bowed down, their faces on the floor.

"Why do you seek the living among the dead?" the men asked. "Remember what he told you when he was still in Galilee, saying that the Son of Man must be delivered up into the hands of sinful men and be crucified, and the third day rise again."

Then the women remembered. Suddenly all the words that Jesus had spoken made sense. They finally understood those things He had told them that had mystified them before.

Their next thought was to tell the good news to the disciples, the Eleven, the ones who were so close to Jesus. The ones who had shared their heartbreak could now share their joy.

Yet the disciples were unbelieving, thinking the women were talking nonsense. Except for one, Peter, who ran to the tomb.

Finding the tomb empty, just as the woman had said, he left that place of death, wondering.

Two disciples, walking along the road to Emmaus, just a few miles from Jerusalem, were joined by the risen Jesus, yet they were kept from recognising Him. As they discussed all that had happened, He shared with them from the Scriptures how Moses and the prophets had pointed to these very happenings and all that was written about Him.

It was not until Jesus sat down to share a meal with them and broke the bread that their eyes were opened, and they recognised Him just before He vanished from their sight. Slow to believe and understand, they realised that as their hearts had been burning within them, it was Jesus who had been speaking with them.

They didn't waste a moment. Keen to share the good news, they headed straight for Jerusalem to find the other disciples. They found them hidden behind locked doors, afraid of what the Jewish leaders might do to them. "It's true. The Lord is risen!" They started to tell the story of their walk, the stranger who had joined them, how He opened the Scriptures to them, and how they finally realised it was Jesus.

As they were speaking, Jesus himself stood among them. Surely this was a ghost! They were startled, afraid, terrified. Seeing their fear and doubt, Jesus spoke reassurance to their troubled minds: "Why are you so troubled? Why do your hearts doubt? Look at my hands and my feet; it's really me. Touch me and see, for a spirit doesn't have flesh and bones, as you can see that I have."

Jesus showed them His hands and feet, yet they thought it was too amazing to be true. To prove that He was really there with them, Jesus ate a piece of fish then opened up the Scriptures to them, helping them to understand all that was spoken about Him in God's Word and how it had now been fulfilled—that it was destined for Him to suffer and to rise from the dead the third day and how repentance and forgiveness of sins should be preached in His name to all the nations, starting in Jerusalem.

Jesus' followers finally understood.
All that He spoke to them came true.
Everything He promised came about.

In one day, everything changed.
They thought it was the end.
It was only the beginning.

Confusion and bewilderment were replaced with wonder and amazement.

The fearful...given hope.
The doubting...filled with faith.
Heavy hearts...now burning within.
The blind...able to see.
Those in mourning...filled with joy.

Happiness displaces heartache.
Understanding replaces confusion.
Hope ousts fear.
Faith takes over doubt.
Joy abolishes mourning.

Reflection

Father, thank you for your amazing rescue plan for me.

I'm in awe at all that you've done for me.

Thank you that the resurrection changes everything.

Thank you for the freedom that you purchased on the cross, for the joy that I can know through you and all the fears you take away.

Thank you that, through You, I can know joy, peace and hope.

CHAPTER TWENTY FOUR

Resurrection Day

"Behold, we are going up to Jerusalem, and the Son of Man will be delivered to the chief priests and the scribes; and they will condemn Him to death and will hand Him over to the Gentiles. They will mock Him and spit on Him, and scourge Him and kill Him, and three days later He will rise again." Mark 10:33–34 (NKJV)

"And if Christ has not been raised, our preaching is useless and so is your faith." 1 Corinthians 15:14 (NIV)

"But God raised Him from the dead ... because it was impossible for death to keep its hold on him." Acts 2:24 (NIV)

"...just as Christ was raised from the dead through the glory of the Father, we too may live a new life." Romans 6:4 (NIV)

"Just as one person did it wrong and got us in all this trouble with sin and death, another person did it right and got us out of it. But more than just getting us out of trouble, he got us into life!" Romans 5:18 (The Message).

R esurrection Day.

Jesus has risen from the dead.
The world is turned upside down.
A new beginning.

Jesus' resurrection quite literally changes everything.
All that Jesus had promised his followers hung on the fact of this unprecedented event in history.

The resurrection was at the heart of Jesus' message, and is the final fulfilment of all that Jesus had spoken about.

The resurrection breaks the final barrier of death. The empty tomb changes everything. Forever. Death is finally overcome. Conquered.

Death was no match for Jesus.

At his resurrection, Jesus is proved to be all that He has said about himself: Messiah, King, Son of God, Holy One. It was the final, unequivocal proof that Jesus is who He said He was.

The resurrection is the final and ultimate demonstration of God's love and "incomparably great power" (Ephesians 1:19, NIV).

In the same way that death came into the world through a man, Adam, so resurrection came through a man, Jesus. This last Adam, Jesus, is a life-giving spirit. (1 Corinthians 15:45 NIV)

He was "delivered to death for our sins and was raised to life for our justification" (Romans 4:25 NIV). He was raised to life to be our High Priest, interceding for us at the right hand of the Father.

In rising from the dead, Jesus defeated death, once and for all.

Jesus' resurrection makes us righteous in the sight of God. No longer sinners unable to approach God, but washed clean and able to enter His holy presence.

This one "wildly extravagant life-gift" (Roman 5:17 The Message) gives us life.

New life.
    Full life.
        Abundant life.
            Eternal life.

Reflection

Thank you for the resurrection. Thank you for the hope it gives me.

Thank you that, though I don't deserve it, you've made me righteous.

Thank you for this amazing gift of life.

CHAPTER TWENTY FIVE

The Final Gift – Shalom

"Glory to God in the highest heaven, and on earth peace to those on whom his favour rests." Luke 2:14 (NIV)

"Peace I leave with you; my peace I give you. I do not give to you as the world gives. Do not let your hearts be troubled and do not be afraid." John 14:27 (NIV)

"For it was the Father's good pleasure for all the fullness to dwell in Him, and through Him to reconcile all things to Himself, having made peace through the blood of His cross." Colossians 1:19–20 (NASB)

"On the evening of that first day of the week, when the disciples were together, with the doors locked for fear of the Jewish leaders, Jesus came and stood among them and said, 'Peace be with you!'" John 20:19 (NIV)

Peace...the one gift that Jesus alone can truly give.

From the song sung by the angels to announce His birth to the first words spoken by the resurrected Jesus to His gathered disciples, we read of this peace, this shalom, that He brings.

Peace is who He is, His identity. He is our Mighty God, Everlasting Father, Prince of Peace.

As Jesus prepared His disciples for His betrayal and death, He entreated them not to be fearful but to receive the peace that He gave them.

Yet this peace did not seem sufficient to see His disciples through the coming days as they ran in fear for their lives.

Following His resurrection, Jesus came again to this fearful group hidden behind closed doors in fear of the Jews. He greeted His astonished followers: "Shalom Aleichem," which means "Peace be upon you."

His first words to them brought them much-needed peace. There was no finger-pointing or recriminations, just His peace. Peace is what He wants to bring to His followers, whatever disappointments or trials they face.

Shalom means so much more than just peace. It means real, complete peace. Peace deep within our souls. Restoration and well-being to our hearts. Wholeness and completeness for our spirits.

Jesus found his disciples locked in an upper room for fear of the Jews, and He brought a gift that met their every need. He fulfilled where they were lacking, restored their relationship, and brought wholeness to their brokenness.

Jesus brought them shalom, perfect peace, certain safety. Shalom, the contentment, blessing, and rest that comes only from fellowship with God.

Through His death and resurrection, Jesus has paid the price and made peace. As the Prince of Peace, peace is His to give.

It's this peace that enabled His once-fearful disciples to live lives filled with courage. It's His power that enabled them to face persecution, rejoice in trials, remain calm through the storms, and conquer the world.

All who place their trust in Him can know this peace of God, that passes all understanding (Philippians 4:17,). His shalom can give us peace as we pass through storms and blessings through the trials and storms of life. With Him, we can be restored, become complete, and be made whole.

His peace, His shalom, can be ours today.

Reflection

Father, thank you that through you I can know peace. Perfect peace.

Father, help me to release my fears to you now. Help me to place my trust in you. Help me to trust in your promises.

Father, fill me with your Holy Spirit.
Restore me; make me whole.
Help me to know your peace as I walk with you.

CHAPTER TWENTY SIX

The Victory Won

"Then I looked and heard the voice of many angels, numbering thou-sands upon thousands, and ten thousand times ten thousand. They en-circled the throne and the living creatures and the elders. In a loud voice they were saying:
'Worthy is the Lamb, who was slain,
to receive power and wealth and wisdom and strength
and honor and glory and praise!'
Then I heard every creature in heaven and on earth and under the earth and on the sea, and all that is in them, saying:
'To him who sits on the throne and to the Lamb
be praise and honour and glory and power,
for ever and ever!'
The four living creatures said, 'Amen,' and the elders fell down and worshiped." Revelation 5:11–14 (NIV)

Jesus returned to the Father and took His rightful place, the place of honour at the Father's right hand.

As the Son returned to the Father, heaven erupted in celebra-tion. The Father declared it, and the angels responded in wor-ship. Thousands on thousands of angels surrounded the throne, singing, worshipping. Those around the throne fell down before Him. All worshipped before Him and cried out in praise.

God raised Him up, lifted him, and honoured Him above all creation—everyone is to bow and worship Him.

Jesus, with all the glory of royalty, yet bearing the marks of death—the death that purchased life for all—still visible in the heavens.

Death is overcome.

This slain Lamb is declared worthy, worthy to open the scroll.
Worthy to receive power, wealth, wisdom, and strength.
Worthy to receive all honour, all glory, and all praise.
He's utterly magnificent. Marvellously majestic. Endlessly excellent. Completely praise-worthy.

The victory's won. He's paid the price and bought a people for himself from every tribe, every language, all peoples and nations.
One day, every knee will bow before Him.
His rule will never end.
His throne will last forever.

The wedding supper of the Lamb is prepared.
The Father promises to make Jesus' enemies a footstool for His feet.
Though war may continue, Jesus' blood on the cross has purchased the eternal victory.
Jesus, Lord of lords and King of kings, will overcome.

Every moment of Jesus' years on earth—worth it.
The pain, the bloodshed, the agony—all worth it.
The betrayal, the anguish, the loneliness—worth it.

Finally, it is finished.
Completed.
The victory is won.

Following Jesus

Have you been touched by the Easter story?

Is it time for you to come to the cross, a place of reconciliation, a place of peace?

Are you ready to become a follower of Jesus?

If you're not sure whether you're truly a follower of Jesus, you can become one now by praying this simple prayer:

Father,

I am sorry for the things I have done wrong. Thank you that Jesus died on the cross for me, rose from the dead, and is alive today.

Forgive me for living life my own way. Please come into my life and fill me with your Holy Spirit.

I accept Jesus as my Lord and Saviour. I choose to follow Him each and every day.

Amen

If you have prayed this prayer, you have been forgiven. Jesus has taken away all the things you have ever done wrong. You are a child of God and have been given eternal life—starting today!

You have begun a new life, strengthened by the power of the Holy Spirit.

What Do I Do Now?

Tell someone – If you know others who follow Jesus, tell one that you trust that you have prayed this prayer.

Find and read a Bible regularly – If you don't have one, either buy one, download a free Bible app, or read it online.

Get involved in a local church – A good church will help you to grow and learn as a follower of Jesus.

Pray – Talk to God, forgive others, and ask Him to supply your daily needs. Thank Him for the good things He has done for you.

About the Author

Jennifer Carter is a child of God.

She's someone who's taken the wrong path but has been saved by God's goodness and grace, rescued by His love and compassion.

She's not a theologian, just someone who believes that the Bible, the Word of God, has the power to change us. That ordinary people can accomplish amazing things with an extraordinary God.

Jennifer is a mother to three grown up children and is also a grandmother. She lives in Salisbury in the south of England.

You can find more about the author and her books online at www.jennifer-carter.com where you can also grab a free copy of one of her books.

One More Thing

If you've enjoyed this book, it'd be great if you'd consider leaving a review, which helps other people to find it and know what to expect when they read it. Thank you.

Bible Copyright Information

Scriptures taken marked (NIV) are taken from the Holy Bible, New International Version ®NIV ®Copyright ©1973, 1978, 1984 by Biblical Inc. ™ Used by permission of Zondervan. All rights reserved worldwide. www.zondervan.com

Scripture quotations marked (The Message) are taken from THE MESSAGE. Copyright © by Eugene H. Peterson 1993, 1994, 1995, 1996, 2000, 2001, 2002. Used by permission of Tyndale House Publishers, Inc.

Scripture quotations marked (NLT) are taken from the Holy Bible, New Living Translation, copyright ©1996, 2004, 2007, 2013 by Tyndale House Foundation. Used by permission of Tyndale House Publishers, Inc., Carol Stream, Illinois 60188. All rights reserved.

Scripture quotations marked NASB are taken from the New American Standard Bible®,
Copyright © 1960, 1962, 1963, 1968, 1971, 1972, 1973, 1975, 1977, 1995 by The Lockman Foundation
Used by permission." (www.Lockman.org)

Scripture quotations marked HCSB®, are taken from the Holman Christian Standard Bible®, Copyright © 1999, 2000,

15688861R00081

Printed in Great Britain
by Amazon